My Heart 2 Heart Girlfriends' book

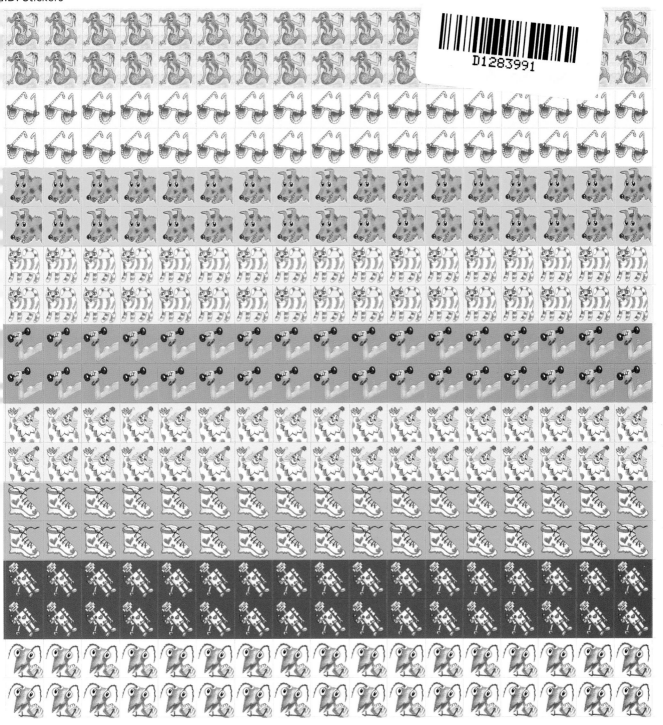

Back Talk Stickers

My Heart 2 Heart Girlfriends' book

I.D. Stickers

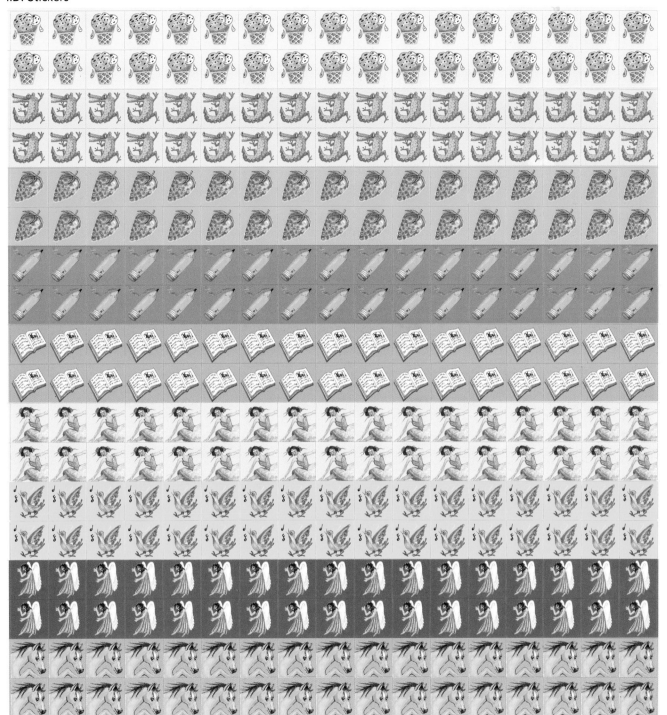

Back Talk Stickers

best place 2 **Hang Out**

my 3 Wishes

best Music

...band...group musician...cd...

Favorite Foods

if U can call it that!

Promise 2 ...

Want 2 B a...

My Room, described in 10 words or fewer

what I Hate 2 Do ! Arggh Yuck

what I'm Reallly Good at

Boys! what about 'em?

my Best Memory

my most **Embarrassing** moment

Me, described in 15 words or fewer

Best Books *(don't forget artists!)* and book characters *(don't forget authors!)*

Best TV Shows and show characters

Best Movies and movie stars

favorite **Sports** ...2 watch 2 play

Best Teachers and why?!
(coaches too)

best Out-of-School activity

best Camp Stuff

make up a **Nickname**

how to Keep a Secret

Hair dos ... 2 wear
2 dare
2 draw

best way 2 **Spend Friend Time**

I like a ☀ 4 a **Pet**, because ...

if I were an **Animal**, I'd be a...

best things about My Family

just don't **Bug-Me** about …